MATH PIRATES
TREASURE HUNT

A LITTLE BOOK OF BIG CHOICES

MATH PIRATES
TREASURE HUNT

BOOK 4: NAVIGATION & MAP SKILLS

S.E. BURR

Copyright © 2021
S.E. Burr
Pirate Illustrations by Mashamashastu
Cover layout and design by Emily Mah

All rights reserved.

No part of this publication may be reproduced, distributed, or transmitted in any form or by any means, including photocopying, recording, or other electronic or mechanical methods, without the prior written permission of the publisher, except in the case of brief quotations embodied in critical reviews and certain other noncommercial uses permitted by copyright law.

Printed in the United States of America

First Printing, 2021

Formatting by:

emtippettsbookdesigns.com

OTHER LITTLE BOOKS OF BIG CHOICES

Math Pirates: The Complete Quest for the Pickled Pearl
(includes the story in this current book you're holding and four others)

Merfriends: The Complete Water Safety Collection

Mage Academy: The Complete Collection

The Adventures of Billy the Chimera Hunter

The Pippa the Werefox Mysteries Volume I
The Pippa the Werefox Mysteries Volume II
The Pippa the Werefox Mysteries Volume III

Learn more about us and get
free ebooks at littlebooksofbigchoices.com

TREASURE MAP

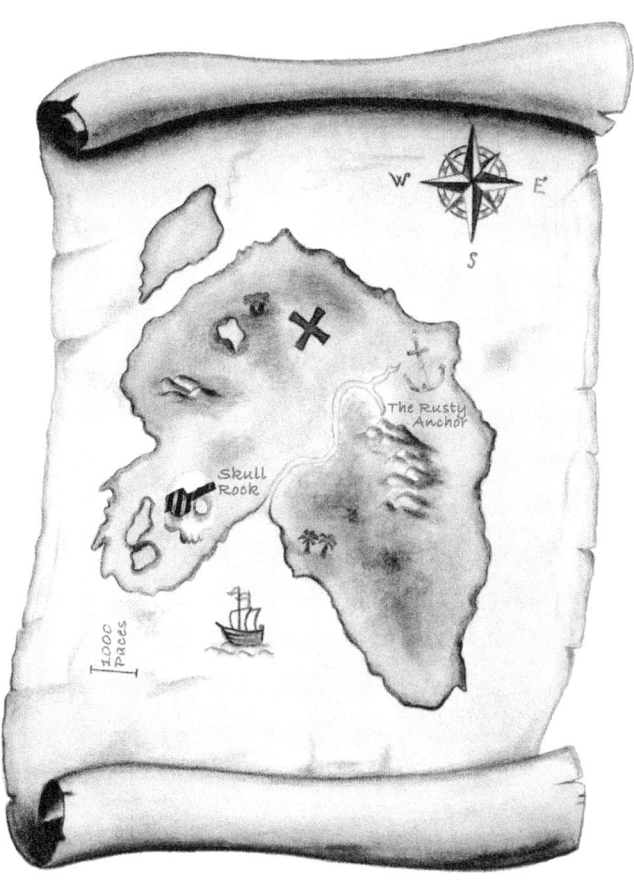

TREASURE HUNT

The crew of the Barnacle Bucket includes six members.

First, there's you, Patrick the Pirate, ship's captain.

Then there are the two mermaids, Marina, your best friend, and McCartney. McCartney is your cousin, she's eighteen years old, she's a mermaid, and she's going to serve as ship's navigator on your voyage. Her father is your uncle, Wade. McCartney's mother and Marina's mother are sisters. So, both you and Marina are McCartney's cousins, but you're not related to each other at all. You're just good friends.

Uncle Six is first mate. He's bald, muscular and exactly six feet tall.

Uncle Wade, McCartney's father, is the helmsman. He steers the ship. He wears a black hat, a fashionable striped shirt, and brown waders—waterproof overalls that let him wade in waist high water without getting wet. He really enjoys wading, and that's why he's called Uncle Wade.

Dr. Fish, Marina's father, is both ship's doctor and ship's cook. He's a tall man who wears fish scale pants.

The journey to the island is pleasant.

There's nothing in the world you like more than sailing. This is the life for you.

One morning after you've been at sea for a few days, you wake early, throw off your blanket, and climb the stairs two at a time, excited to face the day. On deck, you find Uncle Wade, who's on watch, standing at the stern and looking out to sea with a spyglass. You walk over and stand beside him.

He hands you the spyglass. "Take a look," he says.

You do, and at first you see nothing but empty sea and sky, but then you spot something—a distant speck on the horizon. Perhaps it's just a reflection off the water? But you don't think so. "What is it?" you ask.

"A ship," he answers. "We're being followed."

You take a deep breath and then bend

down and give two sharp tugs on the two ropes dangling off the back of the ship.

You and Uncle Wade back away to give the mermaids the space they need. A moment passes and then McCartney leaps from the water and onto the deck. A few seconds later, Marina does the same. They each untie the rope from around their waist. The mermaids prefer to sleep in the water. They tie themselves to the ship so they don't get left behind.

"Good morning, ladies," you say. "Sorry to wake you, but we need to put on some speed." You glance at Uncle Wade out of the corner of your eye. Technically, you're in command of the ship, but Uncle Wade is the more experienced pirate.

He nods in approval. "I'll wake the others," he says.

You sail the ship as fast as you can, but the speck is still there. You can't outrun it.

At local noon, meaning the time when the sun is highest in the sky, McCartney uses her sextant to calculate the ship's position. Local noon is rarely if ever actually 12 o'clock. She uses the mirrors on the sextant to make it appear as though the sun were resting on the horizon and then writes down the time and the angle shown on the sextant. She consults her nautical charts to find your latitude. Latitude is the ship's North / South position. Finding the longitude, the ship's East / West position, requires a more complex calculation, using the sextant to site the moon.

After she's taken your position, the crew sits down together to eat lunch and to discuss the situation.

"We can expect to reach the island

tomorrow," McCartney says.

"We should decide what to do about Percival the Pirate before we get there," you say.

"Are we even sure that it's Percival's ship?" asks Marina. "Maybe it's someone else, or maybe it's just a coincidence that a ship is behind us, and we're not being followed at all."

"Maybe," you say, "but I think it's him. Percival, his daughter Becky, and their parrot Pamela will stop at nothing to get the treasure."

"I agree," says Uncle Six. "Maybe it's not Percival, but it seems too much to hope for that he has given up. I think we need to assume it's him and make a plan to get the treasure and to keep that troublesome trio away from it."

The crew nods.

"Does anyone have any ideas?" you ask.

"I have an idea," says McCartney. "When we near the island, Marina and I will jump overboard and swim to the beach. Meanwhile, the Barnacle Bucket will keep right on sailing, and Percival will think we are just passing by the island on our way to find the treasure somewhere else. You'll sail on for a day or so and then turn back. When we see the ship, we'll swim out with the treasure. You'll pick us up, and then we'll speed back to Pirate Town as quick as we can."

"But how will you get the treasure?" you ask. "It's not on the beach. You'd have to walk to it."

McCartney smiles. "Tomorrow night is the full moon."

"Oh," you say. On the full moon, mermaids' fins turn to legs. "Will you be able to find the treasure at night?"

"No problem," says Marina. "The moon will be full, and besides, we can see in the dark."

"But will you be able to swim out with the treasure?" you ask. "It might be really heavy."

Marina just raises an eyebrow. McCartney scowls at you.

Dr. Fish laughs. "Don't go questioning mermaid abilities, son," he says. "There's nothing stronger than them in the water. Why, Marina's mother fought a great white shark barehanded once, and she won."

Your eyes widen in surprise. "Wow," is all you can say.

Marina gives a pleased smile.

You think of another problem with the plan. "What if we can't find our way back to the island? You're our navigator," you say to McCartney. Around you, the other crew members frown. It would be awful if you got lost and left Marina and McCartney stranded on the island.

McCartney shrugs. "Just keep sailing straight and then sail straight back the other way. The winds have been calm. You'll be able to find the island again easily enough."

"If you say so," you answer. "Any other ideas?" you ask the crew.

"I have an idea," says Uncle Wade. He points to the treasure map. "We'll steer the ship into this bay at the river mouth by Skull Rock. Dr. Fish will row you and Six to shore. Then he'll bring back the rowboat."

"That bay is really far from the treasure," Uncle Six says.

"Exactly!" Says Uncle Wade. "Percival is a pirate, not a tracker. He'll have a much harder time following you on land than on water. You'll walk across the island to find the treasure. Meanwhile, we'll sail the ship around the other side of the island and pick you up here." He points to the northern shore near the X.

"Hmm," you say. "How are we for water?" you ask. "We were planning to refill our empty water barrels at the island. Neither plan allows us time for that."

"We have plenty of water left for the voyage home," says Dr. Fish. "We don't need to refill them."

"What do you want to do, captain?" Uncle Six asks.

Will you send McCartney and Marina to get the treasure (turn to page 12)?
or
Will you and Uncle Six cross the island to get the treasure (turn to page 24)?

You're back on the Barnacle Bucket deciding on a plan to get the treasure. This time you choose McCartney's plan.

MCCARTNEY'S PLAN

You worry about your friends being alone on the island. What if there's some unknown danger, like wild beasts or bottomless pits? What if you have a hard time getting back to the island and you leave them for longer than you agreed? As captain, you prefer to take on the danger yourself, but this plan is both clever and sneaky. Percival the Pirate, his daughter Becky, and their parrot Pamela are brilliant, sneaky pirates. You need to be as clever and as sneaky as possible in order to beat them to the treasure.

Sitting on the deck and looking at the treasure map of the island, you work out the details of the plan with the mermaids.

"We'll approach the island from the east," McCartney says. "With a spyglass, we may or may not see the rusty anchor, but we should be able to see the hills on the eastern side of the island. We'll turn the ship to starboard…"

"To the right," Marina supplies.

"Right, right," McCartney says. "I mean, correct, we'll turn the ship to the right and sail along the northern coast of the island. We'll see the smaller island beside the bigger one. As we get close to the small island, Marina and I will jump into the water on the port side, the left side, of the ship and swim toward that little piece of land north of the X that juts out into the sea."

"Would that be called a headland, or a cape, or a point?" Marina asks.

McCartney takes a long look at the map. "It doesn't really look enough like a peninsula to be any of those. It's not mostly surrounded by water. It's just a little piece of shore that sticks further into the water than the shore beside it. Because it sticks out into the water, we won't have to swim as far."

"All right," says Marina. "How far from the shore is the treasure?"

You cut a little piece of string to be the same length as the scale marked on the map. The scale shows that that length on the map equals 1,000 paces in real life. The center of the X is about two string lengths from the shore.

"About 2,000 paces," you say.

"Whose paces?" Marina asks.

You tap your chin, thinking. "Grandpa Pirate's, I suppose."

"How long is a pace?" Marina asks.

"Hmm," you say. You look at the two mermaids, imagining them with legs instead of fins. You've seen them with legs before, having attended some of the full moon dances they host in mermaid cove. "McCartney, I think you're about the same height as Grandpa Pirate, so your steps would be about the same. You count 2,000 paces from the shore and that should be about where the treasure is."

"Do you think it will be easy to find?" McCartney asks. "I'd hate to have to dig a bunch of holes."

"I think Grandpa Pirate probably marked the spot, maybe with an X on the ground, or maybe it won't even be buried," you say. "This is a quest to prove I'm ready to be a pirate captain. I think sailing to the island and following the map to the treasure are what he's testing, not digging…"

"You think," says McCartney.

"I think," you repeat, "but I could be wrong."

She nods. "Fair enough."

You continue to discuss the plan. "After you two have left the ship, we'll keep sailing westward around the northern side of the island," you say. "Maybe we'll take this channel between the big island and the smaller one?"

"I wouldn't recommend it," says McCartney. "It might be shallow or rocky. You don't want to run aground."

"All right, so we'll go around the little island and then we'll follow the western shore south, past the sand dunes until we get to the inlet on the western shore," you say. "Then we'll turn starboard, right, and start sailing west again."

"And hopefully Percival the Pirate will think you're sailing to something to the west, and you simply had to take a small detour to get around the island," says McCartney.

The next day you enact the plan, and at first it goes off without a hitch. Approaching the island from the east, you can see the rusty anchor and the hills through your spyglass. You turn starboard and sail around the north edge of the island where the mermaids jump off the ship and swim to shore. You continue sailing around the west side of the island where you see the sand dunes and the inlet. You can also see the side of Skull Rock in the distance.

You turn starboard again and continue sailing west. The other ship continues to follow you. You continue sailing west for the rest of that day and into the night.

But then things go terribly wrong. An awful storm kicks up, tossing the ship every which way, and monster waves crash over the sides. You're glad you don't have a chicken coop on deck like some ships do, because if you did, the poor hens would have been washed into the sea within the first half hour of the storm. Your crew is made up of excellent sailors, and you make it through the storm with the ship intact and no one injured, but as the morning dawns, you realize you have no idea where you are. You were supposed to continue straight west from the island, so that you could turn around and head straight east back to it. You don't know where the storm has driven you, but you're sure it's off your intended course. You turn east now to head back toward the island, but you're worried that it may take days to find it.

In the distance you see a white flag and head to it. You find Percival, Becky, and Pamela in a rowboat, the wreckage of what had been their ship floating in the water around them.

You haul them aboard.

"Thanks for the rescue," says Percival.

"Thanks," says Becky.

"Scallywags!" says the parrot.

Becky looks around the deck of your ship. "Where are the mermaids?" she asks.

When you don't answer immediately, Percival's eyes widen and then he gives a knowing grin. "They're back there on that island we passed, aren't they? Retrieving the treasure, I bet." He laughs. "That is a sneaky trick."

"Thanks," you say.

"But you don't know how to get back to the island now, do you?" Becky asks. "Not after that storm. McCartney was your navigator."

You hesitate, but what's the harm in telling them? They're shipwrecked. You've saved them. They have no chance of taking the treasure now.

You nod. "We'll just have to look until we find it," you say.

"Maybe not," says Percival. He squeezes Becky's shoulder. "My daughter is an excellent navigator. She can help you find your way to the island, to the treasure, and to your mermaid friends."

"You can?" you ask Becky.

Before answering, she reaches into her bag and pulls out a sextant, holding it up for you to see. "Sure," she says.

"Great!" you say.

"If you give us each a share of the treasure," she says.

"What!" you say. "But we saved your lives. You're on our ship! We could put you right back in that row boat and let you fend for yourselves on the open ocean!"

"You could," she agrees, "but you won't."

She's right. You won't. You may be a pirate, but you're not a bad guy. "You want two shares of the treasure?" you ask.

"Three," Percival says.

"Three?" you ask.

"One for me, one for Becky, and one for Pamela," he answers.

"Your parrot gets a share!" you exclaim.

"If you accept Becky's help, I'll give up my share," says Dr. Fish. "That way the treasure will be divided into eight shares rather than nine. I'm just anxious to get back to my little girl."

"How about it?" asks Becky.

The entire crew, along with the three new passengers, look at you expectantly.

Will you ask Becky to help you find the way back to the island for three shares of the treasure? The treasure will be divided into eight shares, because Dr. Fish has offered to give up his share. (Turn to page 53.)

or

Will you try to find the island without Becky's help? The treasure will be divided into six shares. (Turn to page 61.)

You're back on the Barnacle Bucket deciding on a plan to get the treasure. This time you choose Uncle Wade's plan.

UNCLE WADE'S PLAN

As the ship's captain, you would rather take a risk yourself than put your friends in danger. You don't know if there is anything dangerous on the island, but if there is, you will be the one to face it.

You sit on the deck with Uncle Six and McCartney and make a plan.

"We will approach the island from the

east," says McCartney. "We should be able to see those hills on the eastern shore with a spyglass."

"What about the rusty anchor?" you ask.

"Maybe, maybe not," she answers.

"Being able to see two different landmarks at once helps you know where you are on a map," you say.

"Right," says Uncle Six, "and so does a shoreline and a compass. It doesn't matter exactly where we are as we approach the eastern coast, because we will not put ashore there. We're going to sail around to the southern coast."

"Correct," says McCartney. "We'll approach the island from the east. Then we'll turn the ship to port(left) and sail south around the southern tip of the island. We'll turn again, this time to starboard (right), and sail into the bay on the southern side of the island. Then you two will get in the rowboat and Dr. Fish will row you to shore. You'll put ashore between the river mouth and Skull Rock. Those are the two landmarks that will let you know where you are on the map."

"Then we'll walk from the shore to where the X is on the map and find the treasure," you say.

"How far is it from the shore to the X?" Uncle Six asks.

You cut a string to be the same length as the scale marked on the map. That distance on the map means 1,000 paces in real life. From the shore to the center of the X is four string lengths. "About 4,000 paces," you say.

"Who's paces?" McCartney asks.

"Probably Grandpa Pirate's," says Uncle Six and frowns. "I'm a little taller than him, so my steps are probably longer than his. You're a lot shorter than him, Patrick, so your steps are probably shorter than his."

"Hmm," you say. "You're a little taller than him, so maybe just take steps that are a little shorter than normal."

He shrugs. "All right. As we're walking, we should be able to see the river to our right and the sand dunes to our left. That's how we'll know we're on the right track."

"And if we get to the northern shore of the island, we'll know we've gone too far," you finish.

"While you're doing that, Dr. Fish will row back out to the Barnacle Bucket and we'll hoist the row boat and him back aboard," says McCartney. "Then we'll sail around the island to meet you on the north shore when you have the treasure."

"Sounds good," you say, and the others

nod.

The next day you enact the plan, and it starts out well. The Barnacle Bucket approaches the island from the east. Using the spyglass. You look straight ahead and see the expected hills. A little to the right, you can see the rusty anchor, too.

Uncle Wade turns the ship to port (to the left) and you sail around the southern tip of the island. You give a wide smile as Skull Rock comes into view.

Dr. Fish rows you and Uncle Six to shore, and that's when the first unexpected thing happens. Instead of turning the rowboat around and heading back to the Barnacle Bucket, Dr. Fish jumps from the boat and pulls it up on shore.

"What are you doing?" you ask.

He doesn't answer. Instead, he strides

forward and examines a tall tree with large leaves and small pink blossoms. "This is a cinchona tree!" he exclaims.

"What?" you ask.

"This tree is medicine!" he says. "The bark of the cinchona tree is what quinine is made from."

"What?" you ask again.

"Quinine is used to treat deadly malaria," Uncle Six says, sounding excited.

Dr. Fish pulls a knife from his belt and begins harvesting the bark from the tree.

"That's great," you say, "but you need to get back to the ship, so you can sail around the island and pick us up when we get the treasure."

"No problem," Dr. Fish says, continuing to cut off bark. "4,000 steps to the treasure, right? That's around two miles. Then another, what? 2,000 steps to the shore while carrying a heavy treasure? I'll harvest this tree and we'll have plenty of time to get to the northern shore to meet you."

"Are you sure?" you ask.

"Sure," he answers, but he doesn't sound sure. He turns briefly and looks at you. "Tell you what, I'll give up my share of the treasure. You can divide it into five shares instead of six. I found my treasure right here," he says, indicating the tree.

"All right," you say, reluctantly agreeing, and you and Uncle Six walk away.

It's a tough walk. The land between the river and the sand dunes is marshy and wet. With each step you take, you have to pull your foot from the mud with a squelch. It's a terrible trudge. Dr. Fish is probably right that he has plenty of time to harvest the quinine before picking you up.

When you've gone about 3,000 exhausting paces, the ground ahead of you looks dry. You see a lovely path of golden sand stretching before you. You and Uncle Six hurry forward and fall into quicksand!

The way the tales tell it, many intrepid young adventurers have met their ends sinking beneath the sands of this particular peril. It's a good story, but not a true one. It's very difficult to drown in quicksand. You and Uncle Six are too buoyant to completely sink, and you can easily keep your heads above the surface.

You won't drown, but you may not get out soon, either. The field of quicksand is huge and there's nothing solid to grab onto anywhere, and you and Uncle Six were already tired out when you fell in.

After at least an hour of struggle, you hear squelching footsteps. "Help!" you and

Uncle Six shout.

The steps get closer and then there's a laugh. "Well Pamela, look at the pickle these two are in," says Percival the Pirate.

"Pickle!" the parrot repeats.

"Are you two all right?" asks Becky.

If it had been members of your crew who found you instead of this tricky trio, you would have asked them for help immediately, but you say, "We're doing just fine, thank you."

Percival laughs again. "Oh, are you?"

"Yes, indeed," you answer.

"You don't reckon you need a little help?" Becky asks. "We've got a long rope. We could pull you from that perilous pit, no problem."

You hesitate. "What will it cost us?" you ask.

"Why, not so much," says Percival, "just one share of your treasure."

"One share?" you repeat.

"Yes, just one for each of us, one for me, one for Becky, and one for Pamela," he says.

"You want a share for your parrot!" you exclaim.

"Yes indeed," he says. "So, what do you say?"

You look at Uncle Six. "It's up to you," he says.

Will you ask Percival, Becky, and Pamela to pull you out of the quicksand for three shares of treasure (turn to page 35)?

or

Will you continue trying to get out of the quicksand on your own (turn to page 44)?

TREASURE HUNT

You and Uncle Six are back in the quicksand and this time you're going to ask Percival, Becky, and Pamela to pull you out.

ASK FOR HELP OUT OF THE QUICKSAND

You decide to ask for their help in exchange for shares of the treasure. Dividing the treasure into eight shares instead of five means that you and each member of your crew will get a lot less treasure. For instance, if the treasure contains 80 gold coins and you divide it into five shares, you each get 16 coins, because 80 divided by five is

16. However, if you divide 80 coins into eight shares, you each only get 10 coins. That's a big difference, but if you don't ask for their help, you might be stuck in the quicksand for a long time, and what if they find the treasure on their own? They don't have the map, but if they keep walking in the direction you were going before you got stuck, they might find it. You don't know if it's buried, well-hidden, or sitting out in plain sight. You just know where the X is on the map.

"All right," you say. "Pull us out, and you can each have a share of the treasure, all three of you." It's ridiculous that the parrot gets a share, but what can you do? Your only other choice is to stay in the quicksand.

They toss you one end of a long rope and Percival and Becky haul on the other end to pull you and Uncle Six from the quicksand. Pamela doesn't help. That parrot doesn't deserve part of the treasure! Oh well...

Past the quicksand, the path quickly becomes drier and easier to walk. Uncle Six forgot how many paces he walked before the two of you fell in. You think you may have to walk to the shore and then count 2,000 paces back, but that turns out not to be necessary. You easily find the not-very-well-hidden treasure chest beneath a few branches. You're glad you offered them the shares in exchange for pulling you out. If you hadn't, they might have found the treasure while you were still stuck in the sand.

You open the lid to reveal shiny gold bars. "Wow," you say. "I thought it would be coins."

Percival scowls, "So did I. How are we going to divide that evenly? he asks. "They'll have to be cut into pieces, so we all get equal shares."

"All right," you answer. "We'll cut them into pieces, then."

"You got a tool for cutting gold on your ship?" Becky asks.

"No," you answer. "Do you?"

"No." she says.

At that, Percival takes the bars from the chest one at a time and counts them. "I'll write up a receipt of how many bars there are, and that you owe each of us a one-eighth share, and then and we can both sign it."

Uncle Six elbows you, "Better make it two receipts," he whispers.

"Draw up two receipts," you tell Percival. "You'll have a copy, and we'll have a copy."

He writes up the receipts and you both sign each of them. "Now I'll take this here gold back to Pirate Town," says Percival, "and get it cut up and divided."

Uncle Six elbows you again, but you don't need his prompting this time. "No," you say. "*We'll* take the gold back to Pirate Town and get it cut up and divided."

Percival scowls again.

"All right," says Becky. "The gold will sail to Pirate Town on Patrick's ship."

"Nay," says her father. "That's madness."

"Nay," says Becky. "It's not. There are three reasons that they should take it back to Pirate Town. First, their crew is bigger than ours, which will come in handy in case sneaky pirates attack."

You stifle a laugh. In your opinion, sneaky pirates are already making off with three shares of the treasure, more if you let them.

Becky goes on. "Second, our ship is faster. We can follow them anywhere. They wouldn't be able to escape us even if they tried. Third, they won't try. Patrick is an honest pirate, if ever I've seen one."

Percival gasps. "An honest pirate!"

"Aye," Becky answers.

"I suppose he has that honest look about him," Percival says. "All right, aye. You take the treasure back to Pirate Town and we'll divide the treasure there. But mind, we'll be following you the entire way. Don't try anything funny."

"Of course not," you say. Then you and Uncle Six carry the treasure to the beach where Dr. Fish is waiting to pick you up in the rowboat. He was right. He did have plenty of time to harvest the quinine. He rows you to the Barnacle Bucket. You immediately set sail for Pirate Town. That evening you have a celebration on board with extra rations and beautiful music. The mermaids are talented singers. Their voices are so lovely, they could make a pirate captain shed a happy tear. Only when no other pirates are looking, mind.

Your decisions worked out well. You've got the treasure, and you're headed home. You've completed Grandpa Pirate's quest, and you'll soon be captain of the Pickled Pearl, the best pirate ship in the seven seas.

This book has four different endings so if you haven't seen them all, you can:

TREASURE HUNT

Go back one step and keep trying to get out of the quicksand without the help of Percival, Becky, and Pamela (turn to page 43).

Go back two steps and send Marina and McCartney to get the treasure instead of going yourself (turn to page 11).

Go back to the beginning and re-read the first scene (turn to page 1).

If you've read all four endings, turn to page 69.

You and Uncle Six are back in the quicksand and this time you're going to keep trying to get out without the help of Percival, Becky, and Pamela.

TRY TO GET OUT OF THE QUICKSAND ON YOUR OWN

You decide to keep trying to get out on your own. Dividing the treasure into eight shares instead of five means that you and each member of your crew will get a lot less treasure. For instance, if the treasure contains 800 gold coins and you divide it into five shares, you each get 160 coins, because 800 divided by five is 160. However, if you divide 800 coins into eight shares, you each only get 100 coins. It's just not worth it. You and Uncle Six are sure to get out of the quicksand, eventually. If you don't make it out on your own, your crew will come looking for you. The tricky trio doesn't have the treasure map, so they probably won't be able to find it on their own.

Percival, Becky, and Pamela walk in a wide circle around the quicksand and then keep going in the same direction you were headed before you fell in. They quickly disappear out of sight.

A couple hours later, you're still stuck and you regret your decision. Quicksand is uncomfortable! You and Uncle Six are both absolutely exhausted, and though you're unlikely to sink, it's probably a bad idea to fall asleep, even if you could. As evening approaches, you hear animal calls in the distance, and you get nervous. What if you're attacked by wild beasts? You won't be able to defend yourself.

You hear squelching footsteps heading toward you, and instead of calling for help, you and Uncle Six grow silent. It might be one of your crewmates, but what if it's an animal coming to eat you?

As the steps grow closer, you turn and look, terrified at what you might see.

It's just Becky. She's carrying a long rope.

"Still in there?" she says. "I thought you might be." She ties one end of the rope around a bush and throws you the other end.

You catch it and start trying to pull yourself from the quicksand.

"Gotta go," says Becky. "Papa's waiting in the ship for me."

"You're going?" you ask, surprised. You're surprised that they would leave without the treasure… Oh, no.

"Yep," she answers. "We found the treasure, no problem. We just walked in the same direction you'd been walking since you got on the island and we walked right into it. The chest wasn't even buried, just hidden under a few branches."

"But that's our treasure!" you say. With the help of the rope, you're slowly making progress at getting out. "That's not fair!"

"Sorry," she answers, "guess you should have taken the deal when we offered to pull you out of the quicksand. Then we'd only have three shares, instead of the whole thing."

"Will you take three shares now and give us the rest?" you ask.

"Sorry," she says, and scampers away.

"How about half?" you call after her.

She doesn't answer.

Once you and Uncle Six are out of the quicksand, you want to go after her, but Uncle Six waves you off.

"We're both exhausted," he says. "We'll never catch her, and besides, she came back and saved us from the quicksand. She didn't have to do that."

"But our treasure!" you say.

He just shakes his head, sadly. "That's the life of a pirate; sometimes you get the treasure, and sometimes someone else does. There'll be other maps and other treasures."

"But I need to find the treasure to prove to Grandpa Pirate that I'm ready to captain the Pickled Pearl. He'll never give me his infamous pirate ship, now!" you say.

"Maybe not," Uncle Six agrees.

The trip back to Pirate Town is somber. You love being at sea, but you're worried about how much sailing you'll be able to do in the future. Without the Pickled Pearl, will you have to get a job at the Pirate Town Farm? You like animals. There are worse jobs, you suppose, but your heart is at sea.

When you're finally back in Pirate Town, you sit in Grandpa Pirate's parlor.

"Well, my boy, you found the map, you got a sail, you provisioned the ship, and you got to the island, but you didn't get the treasure, and getting the treasure was the goal of the quest," says Grandpa Pirate.

"Yes, sir," you say, your head hanging.

"I don't think you're ready to captain such a large and infamous pirate ship as the Pickled Pearl," he says.

"No, sir," you say.

"But cheer up, my boy," he says. "You still have the Barnacle Bucket."

You look up. "I do?"

"You do," he answers. "She's a small ship, but a good one, and she's yours to captain until you're ready to take charge of the Pearl."

"Thank you, sir!" you exclaim.

"You're an able pirate, if a little inexperienced," he says. "You'll find other treasures and prove yourself worthy of the Pickled Pearl in time. I know you will."

"Thank you!" you say again.

Your decisions here had mixed results. You didn't get the treasure and win the Pickled Pearl, but your crew went on a quest and returned home safely. Dr. Fish got the quinine he needs to help lots of sick patients. You will continue to captain the Barnacle Bucket, and you still have the chance to prove yourself worthy of the Pickled Pearl.

This book has four different endings so if you haven't seen them all, you can:

Go back one step and ask Percival, Becky, and Pamela to pull you out of the quicksand (turn to page 34).
Go back two steps and send Marina and McCartney to get the treasure instead of going yourself (turn to page 11).
Go back to the beginning and re-read the first scene (turn to page 1).
If you've read all four endings, turn to page 69.

You're back on the Barnacle Bucket, and you've rescued Percival, Becky, and Pamela. This time you're going to ask Becky to help you find the way back to the island.

ASK BECKY TO NAVIGATE

The tricky trio has asked for three shares, and Dr. Fish has offered to give up his share if you take the deal. If you don't take the deal, you still have to pay his share, so the treasure will be divided into six shares if you don't accept Becky's offer to help, and eight shares if you do. Dividing the treasure into eight shares instead of six means that you and each member of your crew will get less treasure. For instance, if the treasure contains 48 gold coins and you divide it into six shares, you each get eight coins, because 48 divided by six is eight. However, if you divide 48 coins into eight shares, you each only get six coins. But you can't put a price on your friends' health and safety. What if it takes you a long time to find your way back to the island? What if you never find it? What if there are wild beasts or no fresh water? Mermaids are good at finding food in the ocean—shellfish, fish, and seaweed—but what if the island beaches don't have those things? Not all beaches are the same.

"All right," you tell Becky. "Take us back, and you each get a share of the treasure." You think it's pretty silly that the parrot gets a share, but their ship sank, so you can see why they need all the treasure they can get. You feel sorry for them.

Becky isn't able to complete her sextant measurements and navigational calculations until after local noon. When she does, you know you made the right choice asking for her help, because the storm blew you way off course. The island is nowhere near due east of your position. You would have been very lost without her.

As it is, you make it to the northern shore of the island a day later than you had planned. When you first spot the mermaids through the spyglass, you're very relieved. They're all right, and they have a chest with them! They swim out to the ship and leap onboard.

When McCartney sees Percival, Becky, and Pamela on deck, she grabs up a cutlass and looks about to attack.

"It's all right!" you tell her.

"What are these sneaky pirates doing here?" she asks.

You explain.

"We were so worried about you all," says Marina. "I'm so glad the Bucket's all right."

You nod and glance at Becky. She must feel awful that her ship sank.

She gives a small smile. "At least we have our lives," she says, "and three shares of treasure."

Opening the chest, you see it contains gold bars rather than coins. You won't be able to divide it until you can get back to Pirate Town and cut the bars into pieces.

Marina hands a sack to her father, Dr. Fish.

"What's this?" he asks and pulls some tree bark from the sack. His eyes widen. "Quinine!" he exclaims.

"What?" you ask.

"The treatment for deadly malaria," he says. "Where did you get this?"

"There was a cinchona tree on the island," Marina says. "I recognized it from the pictures you've shown me."

"That's wonderful!" Dr. Fish says. "This is more treasure than I could ever have hoped for."

"Good," says Percival, "because you gave up your share of the gold."

"Gold," Pamela echoes.

"And it was worth it," Dr. Fish says, and gives his daughter a hug.

The Barnacle Bucket sets sail for home.

That evening you have a celebration on board with extra rations. You ask the mermaids if they'll sing, but they're tired out from their adventure. You dance a jig for the ship's entertainment instead. Your audience is so moved by your performance that they weep… tears of laughter.

Your decisions worked out well. You've got the treasure, and you're headed home. You've completed Grandpa Pirate's quest, and you'll soon be captain of the Pickled Pearl, the best pirate ship in the seven seas.

This book has four different endings so if you haven't seen them all, you can:

Go back one step and try to find the island without Becky's help (turn to page 60).

Go back two steps and go find the treasure yourself instead of sending McCartney and Marina (turn to page 23).

Go back to the beginning and re-read the first scene (turn to page 1).

If you've read all four endings, turn to page 69.

TREASURE HUNT

You're back on the Barnacle Bucket, and you've rescued Percival, Becky, and Pamela. This time you're going to see if you can find the island without Becky's help.

FIND YOUR WAY BACK WITHOUT BECKY'S HELP

The tricky trio has asked for three shares, and Dr. Fish has offered to give up his share if you take the deal. If you don't take the deal, you still have to pay his share, so the treasure will be divided into six shares if you don't accept Becky's offer to help, and eight shares if you do. Dividing the treasure into eight shares instead of six means that you and each member of your crew will get a lot less treasure. For instance, if the treasure contains 480 gold coins and you divide it into six shares, you each get 80 coins, because 480 divided by six is 80. However, if you divide 480 coins into eight shares, you each only get 60 coins. It's just not worth it. You're worried about your friends, but mermaids are good at taking care of themselves. The map of the island shows plenty of (probably) fresh water, and they can find their own fish, shellfish, and seaweed in the ocean.

You turn the Barnacle Bucket due east and are confident that you'll find the island again within a day.

You don't.

Nor do you find it in three days.

Or four. Your crew tries to get you to reconsider taking the deal. Percival, Becky, and

Pamela won't budge. They won't accept less than three shares, and you refuse to pay that much. You've already looked for four days. Surely, you'll find the island soon.

On the fifth day, Uncle Wade, Uncle Six, and Dr. Fish offer their shares to the tricky trio for Becky's help finding the island. She does the sextant measurements and navigational calculations. The ship is much farther north than you thought. You sail southwest for three days and finally reach the island.

Looking through a spyglass, you don't see the mermaids on the northern shore. You take the rowboat to the island where you find a message written on a rock:

Dear Captain Patrick,

We hope you and the crew of the Barnacle Bucket are well. We know that the storm that hit the island likely also hit the ship. We're very worried about you.

We found the treasure and waited on the beach for a week. We ate the shellfish and seaweed we could find, but it wasn't much. The food on this beach isn't as plentiful as our cove in Pirate Town. We're very hungry. We saw a ship out at sea and signaled to it. We offered the pirates aboard the treasure in exchange for taking us back to Pirate Town. We hope to see you there.

Your friends,

McCartney and Marina.

The journey back to Pirate Town is terrible. The crew is mad at you for endangering Marina and McCartney, and the tricky trio is mad at you for losing the treasure.

When you finally make it back, you can't bear to face Grandpa Pirate. You know he'll never make you captain of the Pickled Pearl now. You hear that McCartney and Marina made it home safely, but you don't go to visit them at the mermaid cove. You're sure they blame you for abandoning them on the island. You get a job at Pirate Town Farm helping Aunt Farmer take care of the animals. You like it well enough. You like animals.

One day, you're mucking out the pigsty, when you hear someone walk up behind you. "Hello, my boy," says Grandpa Pirate.

"Hello, sir," you answer, your head bowed.

"My sister tells me you're doing good work caring for her animals," he says.

"Thank you, sir," you answer.

"I thought it was about time that I come see you," Grandpa Pirate says.

You don't answer.

"Do you want to be a farmer?" he asks. "Are you done with piracy?"

"I'm not cut out to be a pirate captain," you say. "I endangered Marina and McCartney, and I lost the treasure."

He sighs. "Well, I'll be honest, my boy. You made a huge mistake. You're clearly not ready to be a captain… yet, but you could be a part of a crew. You could follow orders instead of giving them. Maybe someday…"

"Maybe someday I'll be a captain?" you ask.

"Maybe," he answers. "Or you can stay here. My sister is getting older. Just like I'm getting ready to retire, so is she. She chose farming over piracy. You could make the same choice."

You nod. "I like animals," you say.

"I know," he says, "but do you still love

the sea?"

You sigh. "I do," you say.

"What do you want to do?" he asks.

"I don't know," you answer.

He pats your shoulder. "Well, you have plenty of time to decide. I'll see you around, my boy."

"See you," you say.

That night you go to see the mermaids. "I'm sorry I left you on the island," you tell them. "I thought I'd be able to find it without Becky's help."

McCartney just sniffs and turns away, but Marina takes your hand. "I forgive you," she says, and you know you're still friends.

TREASURE HUNT

Your choices turned out horribly. At least you like farming. You can still be a pirate if you want to, just not a captain, not for now, anyway.

This book has four different endings so if you haven't seen them all, you can:

Go back one step and ask for Becky's help to find the island (turn to page 52).
Go back two steps and go find the treasure yourself instead of sending McCartney and Marina (turn to page 23).
Go back to the beginning and re-read the first scene (turn to page 1).
If you've read all four endings, turn to page 69.

CONGRATULATIONS!

You've completed the fourth task in your quest for the Pickled Pearl! Whether your final ending was a complete success or required you to spend some time on a crew to get more training, you are now ready to move on to the next task: *Math Pirates: Dividing the Plunder.*

Or, if you would like to read all the stories

about the quest for the Pickled Pearl in one book, they are in *Math Pirates: The Complete Quest for the Pickled Pearl.*

GET FREE BOOKS!

When you sign up for our mailing list at littlebooksofBIGchoices.com, you will receive the first book of every series we write for free. Head on over and sign up today!

littlebooksofBIGchoices.com

ABOUT THE AUTHOR

Once upon a time there were two little girls named Margaret.

One of the Margarets had brown hair and the other had red, and they were both poor and lived on farms, because in those days most little girls were poor and lived on farms.

And when the Margarets got older, they went to college, even though poor girls rarely did, but the Margarets were stubborn and lucky, so they got to go.

Brown-Haired Margaret became a nurse and then a librarian. Red-Haired-Margaret became a school teacher. They spent their lives helping, teaching, and reading.

Who did they help, teach, and read to the most?

Their children, of course.

Brown-Haired-Margaret had a son and Red-Haired-Margaret had a daughter, and that son and that daughter met and fell in love, and together they spent their lives reading, which is almost a happy ending...

But not quite, because what made the story even better, was that the son and the daughter had a daughter of their own and they raised her in libraries and in bookstores and left her to her own devices to play and to wander among the stacks of books, where she found innumerable adventures waiting for her between the pages.

The brown-haired Margaret and the red-haired Margaret both became white-haired-Margarets and they continued to help, and teach, and read.

And who did they help, teach, and read

to the most?

Their granddaughter, of course!

She grew up to love books EVEN MORE, than her parents had. She loved books so much, in fact, that she wanted to make more of them, and because she was stubborn and lucky, she did.

S.E. Burr's greatest desire is to spend her life helping, teaching, and reading like her grandmothers did.

Made in United States
North Haven, CT
30 January 2024

48100019R00050